COMFORT MY PEOPLE

Prayer Services for the Sick and Suffering

by Dorothy E. Bedics

A Campion Book

Loyola University Press
Chicago

Loyola University Press
3441 North Ashland Avenue
Chicago, Illinois 60657

All Scripture excerpts used by permission of publishers.
Unless otherwise noted, scriptural passages are taken from:

THE JERUSALEM BIBLE
Copyright © 1966 by
Darton, Longman & Todd, Ltd.
and Doubleday, a division of
Bantam, Doubleday, Dell
Publishing Group, Inc.

Scriptural text identified (TEV) is taken from:
SING, The Book Of Psalms
Today's English Version
Copyright © 1976
American Bible Society

Library of Congress Cataloging in Publication Data
    Bedics, Dorothy E.
    Comfort my people: prayer services for the sick
    and suffering / by Dorothy E. Bedics.
        p.   cm.
        ISBN 0-8294-0638-7 : $9.95
        1. Sick–Prayer-books and devotions–English.
        2. Catholic Church–Prayer-books and devotions–English.
    I. Title.
    BX2373.S5B43   1990   89-48394
    242' . 4–dc20   CIP

Dedicated to my dear family
and friends in the Lord
who share God's love with me
through their love,
and to the Lord
whose love gives our lives meaning.

CONTENTS

Introduction   vi

1 The Lord Is Close to Us in Our Suffering   2

2 Relying Completely on the Lord for Our Strength 8

3 The Lord Wants Us to be Close to Him   16

4 Depending on the Lord for our Sustenance   22

5 Living in the Holy Spirit   30

6 Our Relationship with the Father   38

7 Our Relationship with Jesus   46

8 The Meaning of Suffering   54

9 Sharing the Lord's Suffering   62

10 Jesus, the Good Shepherd   70

11 Union with Jesus in the Blessed Sacrament   78

12 Recognizing Our Own Beauty and Sharing
    the Lord's Love   86

13 Sharing the Lord's Ministry   96

14 Mary, Our Mother   104

Acknowledgments   112

INTRODUCTION

Comfort My People is a collection of meditations written as a source of spiritual support and consolation for the sick and the suffering. There are fourteen prayer services in this collection, each one is made up of scripture readings and original prayers and reflections centered around individual topics especially relevant to those who are experiencing sickness or suffering in their lives.

I am in a special position to empathize with the needs of the sick and shut-ins, since I myself have been severely disabled, confined to a wheelchair and a shut-in since 1982. These meditations are drawn from my own experience of the need to reconcile the suffering in our lives with our relationship to the Lord. These prayers and reflections are an attempt to share my own experience of the power of the Lord's love to strengthen, comfort, heal and fulfill us, through all the circumstances of our lives. Even in the darkest periods of our lives, we can find support and peace in our personal relationship with the Lord, if we go to him and allow him to love us.

These services can be used for private prayer as well as being used by parishes in their ministry to the sick and suffering. Originally, some of these services were used as part of our parish outreach program to the sick and shut-ins. Eucharistic ministers visiting the sick would pray the prayers with them before giving them the Blessed Sacrament. In either case, these prayers and reflections are designed to foster intimate, trusting communication with the Lord at those times in our lives when we most need him.

1

The Lord
is Close to Us
in Our Suffering

Nothing, therefore, can come between us and the love of Christ, even if we are troubled or worried (sick or suffering), or being persecuted, or lacking food or clothes, or being threatened, or even attacked. . . . These are the trials through which we triumph, by the power of him who loved us.

For I am certain of this: neither death nor life, no angel, no prince, nothing that exists, nothing still to come, not any power, or height, or depth, nor any created thing, can ever come between us and the love of God made visible in Christ Jesus our Lord.

– Romans 8:35-39

Reconciliation

Take this time to share with the Lord everything that is hurting you inside, everything that causes you to feel separated from him. Tell him about each thing one by one, your pain, sickness, fear, anxiety, anger, doubts, sadness. . .

Prayer

Lord, take all these things into your hands and touch them with your healing love. We need to know you are with us. Help us to find you in the center of our suffering as well as in the midst of our joys and comforts. Help us to understand that to surrender ourselves to your will is to surrender ourselves to your love. Help us to trust in your love for us–your love that is even stronger than death. Give us the humility and faith to rely completely on your strength in our weakness. Help us to be aware of your nearness to us, of your holding our hand in the dark, of the power of your love–even when we cannot feel it. Help us to rest in the warmth of your love for us, as a child rests peacefully in its mother's arms.

Scripture Readings

. . .I have loved you with an everlasting love. . .

– Jeremiah 31:3

. . .I have chosen you, not rejected you. Do not be afraid, for I am with you. Stop being anxious and watchful, for I am your God. I give you strength, I bring you help. I uphold you with my victorious right hand. . . . For I am

Yahweh, your God. I am holding you by the right hand;
I tell you,"Do not be afraid, I will help you."

-Isaiah 41:9-10, 13

Does a woman forget her baby at the breast, or fail to
cherish the son of her womb? Yet even if these forget,
I will never forget you. See. I have branded you on the
palms of my hands.

–Isaiah 49: 15-16

Do not be afraid, for I have redeemed you; I have called
you by your name, you are mine. Should you pass
through the sea, I will be with you; or through rivers,
they will not swallow you up. Should you walk through
fire, you will not be scorched and the flames will not
burn you. For I am Yahweh, your God. . . .Because you
are precious in my eyes, because you are honored and I
love you. . . .

–Isaiah 43:2-4

Responsorial Psalm

Psalm 62

R: In God alone there is rest for my soul!

In God alone there is rest for my soul,

from him comes my safety;

with him alone for my rock, my safety,

my fortress, I can never fall.

R: In God alone there is rest for my soul!

Rest in God alone, my soul!

He is the source of my hope;

rest in God, my safety, my glory,

the rock of my strength.

R: In God alone there is rest for my soul!

In God I find shelter,

rely on him,

people, at all times;

unburden your hearts to him,

God is a shelter for us.

R: In God alone there is rest for my soul!

It is for God to be strong,

for you, Lord, to be loving.

R: In God alone there is rest for my soul!

Gospel

"Come to me, all of you who labor and are overburdened, and I will give you rest. Shoulder my yoke and learn from me, for I am gentle and humble in heart, and you will find rest for your souls. Yes, my yoke is easy and my burden light."

– Matthew 11:28-30

Our Father. . .

Communion or Quiet Meditation

After Communion

. . .Let all who are thirsty come: all who want it may have the water of life, and have it free.

– Revelation 22:17

As the Father has loved me, so I have loved you. Remain in my love. . . .

– John 15:9

2

Relying Completely on the Lord for Our Strength

Make your home in me, as I make mine in you. As a branch cannot bear fruit all by itself, but must remain part of the vine, neither can you unless you remain in me.

I am the vine, you are the branches. Whoever remains in me, with me in him, bears fruit in plenty; for cut off from me you can do nothing. . . . Remain in my love.

— John 15: 4-5, 10

Reconciliation

Take time to identify your weaknesses, those areas in your life where you need the Lord's help, those things that cause you suffering; your sickness, pain, fear, anxiety, feelings of helplessness, weariness, loneliness, depression. Share these things with him one by one and ask him for strength and help.

Prayer

Lord, we ask you to reach into these troubles in our lives and touch them; calm them as you calmed the storm on the lake; banish our fear; restore our peace. Lord, we have no strength of our own. We can do nothing without you. We must rely totally on your strength. Help us to trust you. Help us to trust you even in the midst of our weakness and suffering. Help us, Lord, to draw strength from your closeness to us. Give us the grace to accept the things in our lives that we cannot control and to put them into your hands. Help us, Lord, to put ourselves in your hands, and keep us close to you always.

Scripture Readings

For we should like you to realize, brothers and sisters, that the things we had to undergo. . .were more of a burden than we could carry, so that we despaired of coming through alive. Yes, we were carrying our own death warrant with us, and it has taught us not to rely on ourselves but only on God, who raises the dead to life.

– 2 Corinthians 1:8-9

. . .I have pleaded with the Lord three times for (my affliction) to leave me, but he has said, "My grace is enough for you: my power is at its best in weakness." So I shall be very happy to make my weakness my special boast so that the power of Christ may stay over me, and that is why I am quite content with my weakness, and with insults, hardships, persecutions, and the agonies I go through for Christ's sake. For it is when I am weak that I am strong.

– 2 Corinthians 12:8-10

. . .Do not be afraid, do not be daunted by this vast horde; this battle is not yours but God's. . . .Take up your position, stand firm, and see what salvation Yahweh has in store for you. . . .

– 2 Chronicles 20:15,17

. . .In the world you will have trouble, but be brave: I have conquered the world.

– John 16:33

Responsorial Psalm

Psalm 16,25

R: **Protect me, O God; I trust in you for safety.**

Turn to me, Lord, and be merciful to me,

because I am alone and weak.

Relieve me of my worries

and save me from all my troubles.

R: **Protect me, O God; I trust in you for safety.**

You, Lord, are all I have,

and you give me all I need;

my (life) is in your hands.

R: **Protect me, O God; I trust in you for safety.**

I praise the Lord, because he guides me,

and in the night (he instructs) me.

I am always aware of the Lord's presence;

he is near, and nothing can shake me.

R: **Protect me, O God; I trust in you for safety.**

And so I am thankful and glad,

and I feel completely secure,

because you protect me from the power

of death.

R: **Protect me, O God; I trust in you for safety.**

You will show me the path that leads to life;

your presence fills me with joy

and brings me pleasure forever. (TEV)

Gospel

With the coming of evening that same day,(Jesus) said to them, "Let us cross over to the other side." And leaving the crowd behind,(the disciples) took him, just as he was, in the boat; and there were other boats with him. Then it began to blow a gale and the waves were breaking into the boat so that it was almost swamped. But he was in the stern, his head on the cushion, asleep. They woke him and said to him,"Master, do you not care? We are going down!" And he woke up and rebuked the wind and said to the sea, "Quiet now! Be calm!" And the wind dropped, and all was calm again. Then he said to them, "Why are you so frightened? How is it that you have no faith?"

– Mark 4:35-40

Our Father

Communion or Quiet Meditation

After Communion

Ask and it will be given to you; search, and you will find; knock, and the door will be opened to you. For the one who asks always receives; the one who searches always finds; the one who knocks will always have the door opened to him.

– Matthew 7:7-8

Do not be afraid, for I am with you. . . .Because you are precious in my eyes. . .and I love you. . . .

– Isaiah 43:5, 43:4

3

The Lord Wants Us to Be Close to Him

Because of Christ, I have come to consider all these advantages that I had as disadvantages. Not only that, but I believe nothing can happen that will outweigh the supreme advantage of knowing Christ Jesus my Lord. For him I have accepted the loss of everything, and I look on everything as so much rubbish if only I can have Christ and be given a place in him. . . .

— Philippians 3:7-9

Meditation

Take this time to reflect on your relationship with the Lord: that he wants you close to him, to have a special personal relationship with him, to come to know him as a dear, loving friend.

Prayer

We thank you, Lord, for the gift of yourself to us– for remaining with us and making your home with us. Forgive us, Lord, for the times we are not open to your love and will, and for the times we keep you from getting close to us.

Help us, Lord, to trust you. Help us to trust you enough to share everything with you, knowing there is nothing we can't bring to you, nothing we need hide from you, nothing you won't forgive or understand. Help us to share our suffering with you as well as our joy and praise. Help us not to be afraid to share with you how we really feel: our anger, hurt, confusion, sadness, fear, need, thankfulness, love. . . .Give us the grace to be our truest selves in your presence, knowing that you will always love us.

Scripture Readings

"If anyone is thirsty, let him come to me!
Let the person come and drink who believes in me!"

– John 7:38

. . .Anyone who drinks the water that I shall give will never be thirsty again: the water that I shall give will turn into a spring inside him, welling up to eternal life.

– John 4:14

Look, I am standing at the door, knocking. If one of you hears me calling and opens the door, I will come in to share his meal, side by side with him.

– Revelation 3:20

. . . Amen; come, Lord Jesus

– Revelation 22:20

Responsorial Psalm

Psalm 63

R: **God, you are my God and I long for you.**

O God, you are my God, and I long for you.

My whole being desires you;

like a dry, worn out, and waterless land,

my soul is thirsty for you.

R: **God, you are my God and I long for you.**

Let me see you in the sanctuary;

let me see how mighty and glorious you are.

Your constant love is better than life itself,

and so I will praise you.

R: **God, you are my God and I long for you.**

I will give you thanks as long as I live;

I will raise my hands to you in prayer.

My soul will feast and be satisfied,

and I will sing glad songs of praise to you.

R: **God, you are my God and I long for you.**

As I lie in bed, I remember you;

all night long I think of you,

because you have always been my help.

In the shadow of your wings I sing for joy.

I cling to you, and your hand keeps me safe.   (TEV)

R: **God, you are my God and I long for you.**

Gospel

. . . Anybody who loves me will be loved by my Father,
and I shall love him and show myself to him . . . and we
shall come to him and make our home with him.

– John 14:21, 23

As the Father has loved me, so I have loved you. . . .
A man can have no greater love than to lay down his life
for his friends. . . . I shall not call you servants any
more, because a servant does not know his master's
business; I call you friends, because I have made known
to you everything I learned from my Father.

– John 15:9, 13-16

Meditation

Take this time to reflect on the Lord's great love for you,
and tell him of your need for him in your life.

Let us take this time to open ourselves to the special
friendship the Lord wants to have with each one of us.

Our Father . . .

Communion or Quiet Meditation

After Communion

My dear people, since God has loved us so much, we too
should love one another. No one has ever seen God; but
as long as we love one another, God will live in us and
his love will be complete in us.

–1 John 4:11-12

4

Depending on the Lord for Our Sustenance

T
. . . he love of Christ overwhelms us when we reflect that if one man has died for all, then all men should be dead; and the reason he died for all was so that living men should live no longer for themselves, but for him who died and was raised to life for them. . . .And for anyone who is in Christ, there is a new creation; the old creation has gone, and now the new one is here. . . . That is why there is no weakening on our part, and instead, though this outer man of ours may be falling into decay, the inner man is renewed day by day.

– 2 Corinthians 5:14-15, 17; 4:16

Meditation

Reflect on those times that you have shared in the

Lord's suffering. Hold these things out to him trusting

in his love and concern, his desire to comfort and heal

you. Give yourself over to the Lord, allowing him to

nourish, nurture, and sustain you.

23

Prayer

Help us, Lord, to live no longer for ourselves, but for you. Give us a deep, unwavering trust in you; help us to trust you with our lives, even in our sufferings. Stay close to us, Lord. We need you; we need your love and support. Help us to understand that everything you do in our regard you do out of love for us. Unite our sufferings with your own; make us one with you, so that we too may be new creations, renewed, transformed, and sanctified by your love. Help us to put ourselves into your hands so that we may be nourished and strengthened in your care.

Scripture Readings

And the whole community of the sons of Israel began to complain against Moses and Aaron in the wilderness and said to them, "Why did we not die at Yahweh's hand in the land of Egypt, when we were able to sit down to pans of meat and could eat bread to our heart's content! As it is, you have brought us to this wilderness to starve. . .to death!"

Then Yahweh said to Moses, "Now I will rain down bread for you from the heavens. . . . I have heard the complaints of the sons of Israel. Say this to them: "Between the two evenings you shall eat meat, and in the morning you shall have bread to your heart's content. Then you will learn that I, Yahweh, am your God."

– Exodus 16:2-4, 11-12

The poor and needy ask for water, and there is none,
their tongue is parched with thirst.
I, Yahweh, will answer them,
I, the God of Israel, will not abandon them.

I will make rivers well up on barren heights,
and fountains in the midst of valleys;
turn the wilderness into a lake,
and dry ground into waterspring.

– Isaiah 41:17-18

Responsorial Psalm

Psalm 145

R: **Lord, you open your hand and satisfy the desires
of every living thing.**

He, Yahweh, is merciful, tenderhearted,

slow to anger, very loving, and universally kind;

Yahweh's tenderness embraces all his creatures.

R: **Lord, you open your hand and satisfy the desires
of every living thing.**

Always true to his promises,

Yahweh shows love in all he does.

Only stumble, and Yahweh at once supports you,

if others bow you down, he will raise you up.

R: **Lord, you open your hand and satisfy the desires
of every living thing.**

Patiently all creatures look to you

to feed them throughout the year;

quick to satisfy every need,

you feed them all with a generous hand.

R: Lord, you open your hand and satisfy the desires of every living thing.

Righteous in all that he does, Yahweh acts only out of

love, standing close to all who invoke him,

close to all who invoke Yahweh faithfully.

R: Lord, you open your hand and satisfy the desires of every living thing.

Gospel

Jesus said to the people:

"I tell you most solemnly, it was not Moses who gave you

this bread from heaven, it is my Father who gives you

the bread from heaven, the true bread;

for the bread of God is that which comes down from

heaven and gives life to the world."

"Sir," they said, "give us this bread always."

Jesus answered: "I am the bread of life.

He who comes to me will never be hungry;

he who believes in me will never thirst.

I am the living bread which has come down from heaven. Anyone who eats this bread will live for ever; and the bread that I shall give is my flesh, for the life of the world."

– John 6: 32-35, 51

Meditation

Let us reflect on the ways the Lord sustains us in our lives—through our faith, through prayer, through his presence to us, through other people. Let us take this time to try to surrender ourselves to the Lord's tender loving care for us. Let us allow him to nurture us, sustain us and nourish us with himself.

Our Father . . .

Communion or Quiet Meditation

After Communion

"He who eats my flesh and drinks my blood lives in me and I live in him. As I, who am sent by the living Father, myself draw life from the Father, so whoever [feeds on] me will draw life from me."

– John 6:56-57

5

Living in
the Holy Spirit

T

. . . hings that no eye has seen and no ear has heard, things beyond the mind of man, all that God has prepared for those who love him. These are the very things God has revealed to us through the Spirit, for the Spirit reaches the depths of everything, even the depths of God. After all, the depths of a man can only be known by his own spirit, not by any other man, and in the same way the depths of God can only be known by the Spirit of God. Now instead of the spirit of the world, we have received the Spirit that comes from God, to teach us to understand the gifts that he has given us.

–1 Corinthians 2:9-12

Prayer

Dear Lord, fill our hearts with your Holy Spirit of Love, for your Love is our life! Let the touch of your Love be like a healing ointment poured on our wounds. Heal anything in us that needs healing. Bring us to wholeness in body, mind, and spirit. Help us to surrender ourselves trustingly into your hands so that we can rest, peaceful and secure, in your tender embrace. Through the action of your Spirit within us, draw us into a deeper, more intimate relationship with you. Instill in us a fervent love for you so that we can learn to love you the way you want to be loved. Help us to grow closer to you in prayer, holiness and love.

Send us your Spirit to teach us to love. Let our love for one another be guided and directed by your Holy Spirit, that we may learn to love in the purest form possible. Make us one with one another in you. Enable us to be sensitive to the stirrings of your Spirit within us, so that we can serve you faithfully in bringing your love and healing to others.

Scripture Readings

Come close to me, you uninstructed,
take your place in my school.
Why complain about lacking these things
when your souls are so thirsty for them? . . .

Buy her without money, put my yoke upon you

and let your souls receive instruction;

[it is not far off].

– Ecclesiastes 51:23-26

. . . Deep within them I will plant my Law, writing it on

their hearts. Then I will be their God and they shall be

my people. There will be no further need for neighbor to

try to teach neighbor, or brother to say to brother,

"Learn to know Yahweh!" No, they will all know me, the

least no less than the greatest—it is Yahweh who

speaks—since I will forgive their iniquity and never call

their sin to mind.

– Jeremiah 31:33, 34

. . . [The Lord] will be gracious to you when he hears

your cry; when he hears he will answer. . . . He who is

your teacher will hide no longer, and you will see your

teacher with your own eyes. Whether you turn to right

or left, your ears will hear these words behind you, "This

is the way, follow it."

– Isaiah 30:19-21

If you love me you will keep my commandments.

I shall ask the Father,

and he will give you another Advocate

to be with you for ever,

the Spirit of truth

whom the world can never receive

since it neither sees nor knows him;

but you know him,

because he is with you, he is in you.

I will not leave you orphans;

I will come back to you . . .

. . . The Advocate, the Holy Spirit,

whom the Father will send in my name,

will teach you everything

and remind you of all I have said to you.

– John 14:15-18, 25-26

When Pentecost day came round, they had all met in one room, when suddenly they heard what sounded like a powerful wind from heaven, the noise of which filled the entire house in which they were sitting; and something appeared to them that seemed like tongues of fire; these separated and came to rest on the head of each of them. They were all filled with the Holy Spirit, and began to speak foreign languages as the Spirit gave them the gift of speech.

—Acts 2:1-4

Gospel

In the evening of that same day, the first day of the week, the doors were closed in the room where the disciples were, for fear of the Jews. Jesus came and stood among them. He said to them, "Peace be with you," and showed them his hands and his side. The disciples were filled with joy when they saw the Lord, and he said to them again, "Peace be with you. As the Father sent me, so am I sending you." After saying this he breathed on them and said: "Receive the Holy Spirit."

— John 20:19-22

35

Meditation

Take some time now to ask the Lord to send his Holy Spirit into your life, so that through the Spirit he may teach you, guide you, heal you, and reveal himself to you.

Our Father . . .

Communion or Quiet Prayer

After Communion

John baptized with water but you . . . will be baptized with the Holy Spirit.

—Acts 1:5

6

Our Relationship with the Father

Everyone moved by the Spirit is a son of God. The spirit you received is not the spirit of slaves bringing fear into your lives again; it is the spirit of sons, and it makes us cry out, "Abba, Father!" The Spirit himself and our spirit bear united witness that we are children of God. And if we are children we are heirs as well: heirs of God and coheirs with Christ, sharing his sufferings so as to share his glory.

— Romans 8:14-17

Reconciliation

Take some time now to share with Jesus anything that makes it difficult for you to approach the Father — feelings of guilt or shame, inability to trust God, feelings of inadequacy, unworthiness, fear, feeling that God is inaccessible. . . .

Prayer

Dear Lord Jesus, you are the way to the Father. Help us, through our relationship with you, to approach the Father trustingly and unafraid. Heal anything in us that may prevent us from making our home with him and in him. Remove all feelings of fear, guilt, mistrust, or shame from our hearts, so that we can come to know him as a God of love, a kind and loving Father who wishes to draw us protectively and tenderly to himself.

Scripture Readings

Let honesty prompt your thinking about the Lord, seek him in simplicity of heart; since he is to be found by those who do not put him to the test, he shows himself to those who do not distrust him.

—Wisdom 1:1-2

I myself taught Ephraim to walk,

I took them in my arms;

yet they have not understood that I was the one looking after them.

I led them with reins of kindness,

with leading-strings of love.

—Hosea 11:3-4

Ask, and it shall be given to you; search, and you will find; knock, and the door will be opened to you. For the one who asks always receives; the one who searches always finds; the one who knocks will always have the door opened to him. Is there a man among you who would hand his son a stone when he asked for bread? Or would hand him a snake when he asked for a fish? If you, then, who are evil, know how to give your children what is good, how much more will your Father in heaven give good things to those who ask him!

—Matthew 7:7-11

Jesus replied: To have seen me is to have seen the Father. . . . If anyone loves me he will keep my word, and my Father will love him, and we shall come to him and make our home with him.

—John 14:9, 23

Scripture Reading

My dear people,

let us love one another

since love comes from God,

and everyone who loves is begotten by God

and knows God.

God's love for us was revealed

when God sent into the world his only Son

so that we could have life through him;

this is the love I mean:

not our love for God,

but God's love for us when he sent his Son

to be the sacrifice that takes our sins away.

. . . God is love,

and anyone who lives in love

lives in God, and God lives in him.

—1 John 4:7, 9-10, 16

Gospel

Jesus said:

I am the Way, the Truth and the Life.

No one can come to the Father except through me.

If you know me, you know my Father too.

From this moment you know him and have seen him.

I tell you most solemnly . . .

anything you ask for from the Father

he will grant in my name.

Until now you have not asked for anything in my name.

Ask and you will receive,

and so your joy will be complete.

. . . And I do not say that I shall pray to the Father

for you,

because the Father himself loves you

for loving me

and believing that I came from God.

—John 14:6, 7, 12; 16:23, 24, 26-27

Meditation

Spend some time now with God the Father. Ask Jesus to help you approach him. Rest in his deep and tender love for you. Let the power of God's love protect you and fill you with peace. Tell the Father about the things that are troubling you or causing you suffering. Ask him for what you need. Pray for your loved ones. Take some time to thank and praise the Father—for giving us Jesus, for our loved ones, for the good and beauty in our lives.

Our Father . . .

Communion or Quiet Prayer

After Communion

. . . Father, may they be one in us, as you are in me and I am in you.

—John 17:21

7

Our Relationship
with Jesus

... **W**e are ambassadors for Christ; it is as though God were appealing through us, and the appeal that we make in Christ's name is: be reconciled to God. For our sake God made the sinless one into sin, so that in him we might become the (very holiness) of God.

–2 Corinthians 5:20-21

Reconciliation

Let us take this time to think about our personal relationship with the Lord, to reflect on those things inside of us that prevent us from being one with him, those things that prevent us from giving ourselves to him completely, those things that disturb our peace with him.   Let us reflect on our poverty: our inability to trust and love the Lord enough, our weakness, the times we are not open to him, the times we do not allow him to come close to us, the times we resist his guidance, direction, and support in our lives.

Prayer

Dear Lord, heal those things in us that prevent us from surrendering ourselves totally to you. Help us to respond to your love for us, to the close relationship you want to have with each one of us. Let your perfect love for us cast out all our fears. Let your love be our strength and sustaining force. Forgive us for the times we distance ourselves from you. Give us the grace to put our lives in your hands, to rest securely in your care. Enable us to trustingly give ourselves to you as you give yourself to us. Hold us in your love and make us one with you in mind and heart.

Scripture Readings

I will betroth you to myself for ever,
betroth you with integrity and justice,
with tenderness and love;
I will betroth you to myself with faithfulness,
and you will come to know Yahweh.

—Hosea 2:21

The nations then will see your integrity . . . and you will be called by a new name, one which the mouth of Yahweh will confer. You are to be a crown of splendor in the hand of Yahweh, a princely diadem in the hand of your God; no longer are you to be named "Forsaken," nor your land "Abandoned," but you shall be called "My Delight" and your land "The Wedded"; for Yahweh takes delight in you and your land will have its wedding. Like a young man marrying a virgin, so will the one who built you wed you, and as the bridegroom rejoices in his bride, so will your God rejoice in you.

—Isaiah 62:2-5

Do not let your hearts be troubled. Trust in God still, and trust in me. . . . I will not leave you orphans; I will come back to you. I shall ask the Father and he will give you another Advocate to be with you for ever, the Spirit of truth . . . I have said these things to you while still with you; but the Advocate, the Holy Spirit, whom the Father will send in my name, will teach you every-thing and remind you of all I have said to you. Peace I bequeath to you, my own peace I give you, a peace the world cannot give, this is my gift to you.

— John 14:1, 18, 16-17, 25-27

Responsorial Psalm

Psalm 27

R: I love you, Lord; my life is in your hands.

My heart has said of you,

"Seek his face."

Yahweh, I do seek your face;

do not hide your face from me.

R: I love you, Lord; my life is in your hands.

Hear me, Lord, when I call to you!

Be merciful and answer me!

When you said, "Come to me,"

I answered, "I will come, Lord."

Don't hide yourself from me! (TEV)

R: I love you, Lord; my life is in your hands.

Come back to me with all your heart . . .

for I am all tenderness and compassion.

The nearer you go to God,

the nearer he will come to you. . . .

R: I love you, Lord; my life is in your hands.

— James 4:8, Joel 2:12, 13

Gospel

One of the scribes . . . put a question to Jesus, "Which is the first of all the commandments?" Jesus replied, "This is the first: Listen, Israel, the Lord our God is the one Lord, and you must love the Lord your God with all your heart, with all your soul, with all your mind and with all your strength. The second is this: You must love your neighbor as yourself. There is no commandment greater than these."

—Mark 12:28-31

Prayer

O most gentle Jesus, open our hearts to receive your love. Stay close to us, Lord, for we need you. Let the touch of your love move us to a deep, passionate love for you. Instill in us a growing devotion to the gift of yourself in the Blessed Sacrament. Help us to give our hearts to you in intimate, joyful trust. Make our hearts one with your Sacred Heart. Make our will one with your will. Help us to give our lives to you so that we can serve you faithfully in bringing your love to others.

Our Father . . .

Communion or Quiet Prayer

After Communion

As the Father has loved me, so I have loved you.

Remain in my love.

— John 15:9

8

The Meaning of Suffering

Bow down, then, before the power of God now, and he will raise you up on the appointed day; unload all your worries onto him, since he is looking after you. . . . [Remember] that your brothers and sisters all over the world are suffering the same things. You will have to suffer only for a little while: the God of all grace who called you to eternal glory in Christ will see that all is well again: he will confirm, strengthen and support you. His power lasts for ever and ever. Amen.

—1 Peter 5:6-7, 9-11

Reflection

In times of sickness, grief or affliction we are often tempted to believe that God is the cause of our suffering, that our suffering is "God's will," or a punishment for our sins. We become hurt, angry and disillusioned with the Lord. We wonder if he really loves us, if he has forgotten us, or abandoned us in our unworthiness. We become alienated from the Lord when we need him the most.

55

We will never be able to trust the Lord, if we believe he would do anything to hurt us. God loves us. He would never do anything to harm us. The Lord does not inflict us with pain and suffering. He does not want to hurt us, or punish us, or deprive us. He just wants to love us! He wants to put his arms around us and comfort us in our distress.

Reconciliation

Take some time now to share with the Lord everything that is hurting you—your suffering, your sickness, your fears, your inability to trust the Lord, feelings of abandonment, anger, disillusionment, helplessness, despair. Open your heart to the Lord. Tell him exactly how you feel deep down inside. Ask him about the things that trouble you or cause you to lose faith. He is longing to share your suffering with you—to unburden your heart in his Heart, to show you how much he loves you. Spend some time resting in the Lord's love, asking his healing and forgiveness.

Prayer

Dear Lord, we bring you our burdens, our fears, our suffering. We bring you our anger, our weakness, our doubts, our lack of trust in you. Remove all bitterness from our hearts. Heal any feelings of guilt or blame—blaming you for our afflictions or blaming ourselves. Reconcile anything in us that alienates us from you, from ourselves, or from one another. Stay close to us, Lord; we need you. We need to know you love us and are taking care of us. Help us to trust you, through all the circumstances of our lives. Give us the strength and courage to endure. Keep us safe and secure in your tender embrace. Fill our lives with the peace that only your Love can bring, that peace that overcomes our darkness.

Scripture Reading

Death was not God's doing, he takes no pleasure
in the [destruction] of the living.
To be—for this he created all;
the world's created things have health in them. . . .

Yet God did make man imperishable,

he made him in the image of his own nature;

it was the devil's envy that brought death into the world,

as those who are his partners will discover.

—Wisdom 1:13-14, 2:23-24

Responsorial Psalm

Psalm 103

R: **The Lord is close to the brokenhearted;
those who are crushed in spirit he saves.**
—Psalm 34

Bless Yahweh, my soul,

and remember all his kindnesses:

in forgiving all your offenses,

in curing all your diseases,

in redeeming your life from the pit,

in crowning you with love and tenderness.

R: **The Lord is close to the brokenhearted;
those who are crushed in spirit he saves.**

Yahweh, who does what is right,

is always on the side of the oppressed.

Yahweh is tender and compassionate,

slow to anger, most loving;

he never treats us, never punishes us,

as our guilt and our sins deserve.

**R: The Lord is close to the brokenhearted;
those who are crushed in spirit he saves.**

As tenderly as a father treats his children,

so Yahweh treats those who fear him;

he takes our sins, farther away

than the east is from the west.

**R: The Lord is close to the brokenhearted;
those who are crushed in spirit he saves.**

Scripture Reading

. . . God is love and anyone who lives in love lives in
God, and God lives in him. In love there can be no fear,
but fear is driven out by perfect love; because to fear is
to expect punishment, and anyone who is afraid is still
imperfect in love.

Only by this can we be certain that we are children of
the truth and be able to quiet our conscience in his
presence, whatever accusations it may raise against us,

because God is greater than our conscience and he knows everything. My dear people, if we cannot be condemned by our own conscience, we need not be afraid in God's presence. . . .

—1 John 4:16, 18; 3:19-22

Gospel

As Jesus went along, he saw a man who had been blind from birth. His disciples asked him, "Rabbi, who sinned, this man or his parents, for him to have been born blind?" "Neither he nor his parents sinned," Jesus answered, "he was born blind so that the works of God might be displayed in him."

— John 9:1-3

Our Father . . .

Communion or Quiet Prayer

After Communion

Jesus said, "Do not be afraid, only have faith. . . . Do not let your hearts be troubled. Trust in God still, and trust in me. . . . In the world you will have trouble, but be brave: I have conquered the world."

— Luke 8:50, John 14:1, 16:33

9

Sharing the Lord's Suffering

Since in Jesus, the Son of God, we have the supreme high priest who has gone through to the highest heaven, we must never let go of the faith that we have professed. For it is not as if we had a high priest who was incapable of feeling our weaknesses with us; but we have one who has been tempted in every way that we are, though he is without sin. Let us be confident, then, in approaching the throne of grace, that we shall have mercy from him and find grace when we are in need of help.

— Hebrews 4:14-16

Meditation

Take a few moments to come close to the Lord. Spend some time resting in his love for you. Share anything with him that may be an obstacle to your peaceful intimacy with him. Approach the Lord, realizing that he has himself suffered everything we suffer. He knows what we are going through. He looks upon us with tender sympathy and understanding. Ask the Lord to heal anything in you that needs healing. Tell him about your needs. Offer him your suffering. Thank him for his gifts. Express your love for him.

Prayer

Dear Jesus, you reconciled us to yourself through your own suffering. You gave your life, that we may have life in you. You so ardently desired to be one with us, you died to make that possible. Enable us to experience your burning love for us, that love that led you to be wounded for our sakes. Let the suffering in our own lives serve not to separate us from you, but to draw us into an ever deepening union with you, through the power of your sanctifying grace.

Dear Lord, your sacrifice of love has broken forever the power of sin and darkness over us. Nothing can ever separate us from you again, if we but come to you. We need only to let you love us. Your love will do the rest. We offer you our hearts. We offer you our lives.

We offer you ourselves. Help us to identify our suffering with your own. Give us the grace to accept the hardships and cares of life out of love for you, and in union with you. Unite our suffering to your own so that we may find strength and solace in your embrace. Help us to grow in love and devotion for you. Keep us close to you and make us one with one another in your love.

Scripture Readings

Christ has reconciled you, by his death and in [his own] body. Now you are able to appear before him holy, pure and blameless—as long as you persevere and stand firm on the solid base of the faith, never letting yourself drift away from the hope promised by the Good News, which you have heard, which has been preached to the whole human race. . . . It makes me happy to suffer for you, as I am suffering now, and in my own body to do what I can to make up all that has still to be undergone by Christ for the sake of his body, the Church.

— Colosians 1:22-24

You will have in you the strength, based on his own glorious power, never to give in, but to bear anything joyfully, thanking the Father who has made it possible for you to join the saints and with them to inherit the light. . . . He has taken us out of the power of darkness and created a place for us in the kingdom of the Son that he loves, and in him, we gain our freedom, the forgiveness of our sins.

—Colosians 1:11-14

Responsorial Psalm

1 Peter 2:21-24

R: By his wounds we were healed.

. . . Christ suffered for you

and left an example

for you to follow the way he took.

He had not done anything wrong,

and there had been no perjury in his mouth.

He was insulted

and did not retaliate with insults.

R: By his wounds we were healed.

When he was tortured

he made no threats,

but he put his trust

in the righteous judge.

He was bearing our faults

in his own body on the cross,

so that we might die to our faults

and live for holiness.

R: By his wounds we were healed.

Gospel

James and John, the sons of Zebedee, approached him
. . . and said to him, "Allow us to sit one at your right
hand and the other at your left in your glory." "You do
not know what you are asking," Jesus said to them.
"Can you drink the cup that I must drink, or be baptised
with the baptism with which I must be baptised?" They
replied, "We can." Jesus said to them, "The cup that I

must drink, you shall drink, and with the baptism with which I must be baptised you shall be baptised, but as for seats at my right hand or my left, these are not mine to grant; they belong to those to whom they have been allotted."

—Mark 10:35-40

Reflection

When we try to stay close to the Lord, regardless of the pain and suffering we encounter in our lives, we are already sharing his cup. We share in the Lord's suffering, as he has shared in ours. We can commiserate with him in mutual sympathy and love. His grace makes this possible. When we offer our suffering to the Lord, our suffering, in union with Christ's, can have redemptive value. We can offer our suffering as prayers for others, thereby participating with Christ in the salvation of ourselves, our family, our friends, our loved ones, and even the whole world.

Our Father . . .

Communion or Quiet Prayer

After Communion

...I have been crucified with Christ, and I live now not with my own life, but with the life of Christ who lives in me. The life I now live in this body I live in faith: faith in the Son of God, who loved me and who sacrificed himself for my sake.

— Galatians 2:19-20

10

Jesus, the Good Shepherd

For the Lord Yahweh says this: I am going to look after my flock myself and keep all of it in view. As a shepherd keeps all his flock in view when he stands up in the middle of his scattered sheep, so shall I keep my sheep in view. I shall rescue them from wherever they have been scattered during the mist and darkness. . . . I myself will pasture my sheep, I myself will show them where to rest—it is the Lord Yahweh who speaks. I shall look for the lost one, bring back the stray, bandage the wounded and make the weak strong. . . . I shall be a true shepherd to them.

—Ezekiel 34:11-12, 15-16

Prayer

Just as a mother nourishes her precious baby with life-giving sustenance, you too, Lord Jesus, nourish us with yourself. You sustain us with your own life in the Blessed Sacrament. You nurture us with your loving presence within us. You tenderly communicate your

71

love to us—in our prayer, through your Word, through our relationships, and through your action in our lives.

Dear Lord, you never wait for us to come to you. When we are too tired or too weak to come to you, you come to us! You search us out and pursue us, until you hold us once again in your comforting embrace. Help us to recognize your gentle voice when you call. We bring you our wounds, our suffering, our sinfulness. Wrap us in your love and heal us with your merciful touch. Draw us closer to yourself and remove all obstacles to trusting intimacy with you. Lead us to rest peacefully in your arms, and to grow in love for you and for each other.

Scripture Reading

I tell you most solemnly,
I am the gate of the sheepfold.
All others who have come
are thieves and brigands;
but the sheep took no notice of them.
I am the gate.

Anyone who enters through me will be safe;

he will go freely in and out

and be sure of finding pasture. . . .

I have come

so that they may have life

and have it to the full.

I am the good shepherd:

the good shepherd is one who lays down his life for his

sheep. . . .

I am the good shepherd;

I know my own

and my own know me,

just as the Father knows me

and I know the Father;

and I lay down my life for my sheep.

— John 10:7-12, 14-15

73

Responsorial Psalm

Psalm 23

**R: The Lord is my shepherd; he gives me everything
I need.**

Yahweh is my shepherd, I lack nothing.

In meadows of green grass he lets me lie.

To the waters of repose he leads me;

there he revives my soul.

He guides me by paths of virtue

for the sake of his name.

Though I pass through a gloomy valley,

I fear no harm;

beside me your rod and your staff

are there, to hearten me.

**R: The Lord is my shepherd; he gives me everything
I need.**

You prepare a table before me

under the eyes of my enemies;

You anoint my head with oil,

my cup brims over.

Ah, how goodness and kindness pursue me,

every day of my life;

my home, the house of Yahweh,

as long as I live!

R: The Lord is my shepherd; he gives me everything I need.

"Console my people, console them" says your God.

Here is the Lord Yahweh coming with power,

his arm subduing all things to him.

He is like a shepherd feeding his flock,

gathering lambs in his arms,

holding them against his breast

and leading to their rest the mother ewes.

—Isaiah 40:1, 10-11

Gospel

What man among you with a hundred sheep, losing one,
would not leave the ninety-nine in the wilderness and go
after the missing one till he found it? And when he
found it, would he not joyfully take it on his shoulders
and then, when he got home, call together his friends
and neighbors? "Rejoice with me," he would say, "I have
found my sheep that was lost." In the same way, I tell
you, there will be more rejoicing in heaven over one
repentant sinner than over ninety-nine virtuous men
who have no need of repentance.

— Luke 15:4-7

Our Father . . .

Communion or Quiet Prayer

After Communion

My refuge, my fortress, my God in whom I trust!
He covers you with his wings and you will be safe in his
embrace.

—Psalm 91:2, 4*
*paraphrased

11

Union with Jesus in the Blessed Sacrament

...**T**hrough our Lord Jesus Christ, by faith we are judged righteous and at peace with God, since it is by faith and through Jesus that we have entered this state of grace in which we can boast about looking forward to God's glory. . . . This hope is not deceptive, because the love of God has been poured into our hearts by the Holy Spirit which has been given us. We were still helpless when at his appointed moment Christ died for sinful men. It is not easy to die even for a good man . . . but what proves that God loves us is that Christ died for us while we were still sinners. Having died to make us righteous, is it likely that he would now fail to save us . . . ? When we were reconciled to God by the death of his Son, we were still enemies; now that we have been reconciled, surely we may count on being saved by the life of his Son. Not merely because we have been reconciled but because we are filled with joyful trust in God, through our Lord Jesus Christ, through whom we have already gained our reconciliation.

—Romans 5:1-2, 5-1

79

Meditation

The Lord so ardently desired to live in loving union with us that he suffered and died to make this possible. He does, however, respect our free will. He urgently pursues us, but he will not force himself upon us. He is seeking us out before we even begin to look for him. He longs to give himself to us in love. We need only let him find us.

Reconciliation

Take a few moments to share with the Lord anything inside of you that prevents you from coming closer to him, anything that causes you to hide from him or avoid living in deeper intimacy with him. Ask his forgiveness for the times you take him for granted, turn away from him, or keep him at arm's length. Ask him to help you give yourself to him, freely and without reserve, as he gives himself to us.

Scripture Reading

Jesus answered: "I tell you most solemnly, it was not Moses who gave you bread from heaven, it is my Father who gives you the bread from heaven, the true bread; for the bread of God is that which comes down from heaven and gives life to the world."

"Sir," they said, "give us that bread always." Jesus answered: "I am the bread of life. He who comes to me will never be hungry; he who believes in me will never thirst. I am the living bread which has come down from heaven. Anyone who eats this bread will live for ever; and the bread that I shall give is my flesh, for the life of the world."

— John 6:32-35, 51

Responsorial Psalm

John 6:53-56

R: Lord, give us this bread always.

"If you do not eat the flesh of the Son of Man

 and drink his blood,

you will not have life in you."

R: Lord, give us this bread always.

"Anyone who does eat my flesh and drink my

blood has eternal life,

and I shall raise him up on the last day."

R: Lord, give us this bread always.

"For my flesh is real food

and my blood is real drink.

He who eats my flesh and drinks my blood

lives in me

and I live in him."

R: Lord, give us this bread always.

Gospel

When evening came Jesus was at table with the twelve disciples. Now as they were eating, Jesus took some bread, and when he had said the blessing he broke it and gave it to the disciples. "Take it and eat," he said, "this is my body." Then he took a cup, and when he had returned thanks he gave it to them. "Drink all of you from this," he said, "for this is my blood, the blood of the [new] covenant, which is to be poured out [for you and] for many for the forgiveness of sins. . . . Do this [in remembrance] of me."

—Matthew 26:20, 26-28; Luke 22:19

Prayer

Come, Lord Jesus. Make your home in our hearts. Even though the dwelling place we offer you is poor and unworthy, we know you do not mind. Your presence, your touch will heal us. Forgive us for the times we withhold ourselves from you. Fill our emptiness with yourself. Heal our brokenness with your love. Calm our fears with your peace, for "our hearts are restless until they rest in you." (St. Augustine)

Meditation

Open yourself to receive the Lord Jesus into your heart, knowing that he longs to give himself to you. Bare your soul before him, as he reveals himself to you. Share with him your deepest thoughts, your deepest desires, your deepest needs, your deepest dreams. Offer yourself to him, realizing his deep love and desire for you. Place yourself in his hands and rest in his gentle embrace.

Our Father . .

Communion or Quiet Prayer

After Communion

"As I, who am sent by the living Father, myself draw life from the Father,
so whoever eats my [Body and drinks my Blood] will draw life from me."

— John 6:57

12

Recognizing Our Own Beauty and Sharing the Lord's Love

s the crowds were appalled on seeing him—so disfigured did he look that he seemed no longer human. . . .Without beauty, without majesty (we saw him), no looks to attract our eyes; a thing despised and rejected by men, a man of sorrows and familiar with suffering, a man to make people screen their faces; he was despised and we took no account of him.

And yet ours were the sufferings he bore, ours the sorrows he carried. But we, we thought of him as someone punished, struck by God, and brought low. Yet he was pierced through for our faults, crushed for our sins. On him lies a punishment that brings us peace, and through his wounds we are healed.

—Isaiah 52:14; 53:2-5

Reconciliation

Take a few moments to come into the Lord's loving presence. Share with the Lord anything that prevents you from feeling good about yourself, anything that detracts from your feelings of self-worth or self-esteem, anything that makes you feel unattractive or unworthy of love.

Tell the Lord about anything that may make you feel unwanted, unloved, isolated, alone, rejected, abandoned or unworthy—in your relationship with him or others. Place before the Lord anything that hinders you from loving yourself, receiving the Lord's love or the love of others. Share with the Lord anything that prevents you from trusting the Lord and surrendering yourself to him.

Meditation

God loves us and cherishes us as we are. He formed us in his own image. "Then God looked at all he had made and saw that it was very good."* We need not be ashamed of our scars, our weaknesses or our infirmities.

Jesus himself shared our infirmities with us. He too experienced the disfigurement of suffering, the helplessness of human frailty. He too suffered sorrow, scorn, and feelings of rejection. If anything, our scars and our woundedness make us even more precious and more beautiful, because they make us resemble our dear Lord in his suffering.

Take some time now to offer your suffering to the Lord. Ask him to unite your scars and wounds with his own. Let his love enfold you. Let him touch you and heal you.

– Genesis 1:31
paraphrased

Scripture Readings

God said, "Let us make man in our own image, in the likeness of ourselves, and let them be masters of the fish of the sea, the birds of heaven, the cattle, all the wild beasts and all the reptiles that crawl upon the earth."

God created man in the image of himself,

in the image of God he created him,

male and female he created them.

God blessed them, saying to them, "Be fruitful, multiply,
fill the earth and conquer it." . . . God saw all he had
made, and indeed it was very good. . . .

— Genesis 1:26-28, 31

. . . I want to urge you in the name of the Lord, not to go
on living the aimless kind of life that pagans live.
Intellectually they are in the dark, and they are
estranged from the life of God, without knowledge
because they have shut their hearts to it. . . . You must
give up your old way of life; you must put aside your old
self, which gets corrupted by following illusory desires.
Your mind must be renewed by a spiritual revolution so
that you can put on the new self that has been created
in God's way, in the goodness and holiness of the truth.

— Ephesians 4:17-18, 22-24

Reflection

The Lord's final request of us before he died was that we should love—love God and love one another. It is love that gives our lives meaning. Without it, life can be a desert wasteland, empty and without hope or joy. We will not, however, be capable of giving or receiving this love until we are able to first love ourselves. We will not be able to accept the Lord's love in our lives if we feel undeserving or unworthy to be loved.

The Lord calls each of us to participate in the love of his Holy Trinity. We are all called to share his love with one another. The Lord can love us through each other and we can love the Lord through each other. Let us ask the Lord to fill us with the warmth of his love and to heal anything in us that prevents us from sharing in his beautiful gift of love.

Prayer

Dear Lord, we were created in your own image and likeness, formed in the depth and power of your love. We thank you for the gift of ourselves, the gift of life. We praise you for breathing your life within us. Help us to see ourselves the way you see us. Give us the grace to grow in appreciation of ourselves and to recognize our own beauty, the beauty you instilled in us, from the moment of our birth. Enable us to be comfortable with ourselves, to love ourselves as you love us, the way we are.

Lord, give us a true sense of our own self-worth and self-esteem so that we will be free to accept your love and the love of others. Draw us into the life of your Blessed Trinity. Banish the loneliness and isolation in our lives and make us one with our spiritual family in you. Fill our hearts with your burning love so that we can love others as you love us.

Responsorial Psalm

The Song of Songs 7:12-13; 8: 6-7

R: **Under his eyes I have found true peace.**

Come, my Beloved...

Then I shall give you

the gift of my love . . .

R: **Under his eyes I have found true peace.**

Set me like a seal on your heart . . .

For love is [stronger than] Death . . .

The flash of it is a flash of fire,

a flame of Yahweh himself.

R: **Under his eyes I have found true peace.**

Love no flood can quench,

no torrents drown.

Were a man to offer

all the wealth of his house to buy love,

contempt is all he would purchase.

R: **Under his eyes I have found true peace.**

Gospel

When [Judas] had gone [to betray Jesus], Jesus said:

"Now has the Son of Man been glorified,

and in him God has been glorified . . .

"My little children,

I shall not be with you much longer . . .

I give you a new commandment:

love one another;

just as I have loved you,

you also must love one another.

By this love you have for one another,

everyone will know that you are my disciples."

— John 13:31, 33-35

Our Father . . .

Communion Prayer

After Communion

As the Father has loved me, so I have loved you.

Remain in my love . . .

– John 15:9

. . . . God is love and anyone who lives in love lives in God, and God lives in him.

– 1 John 4:16

13

Sharing the Lord's Ministry

I, the prisoner in the Lord, implore you therefore to lead a life worthy of your vocation. Bear with one another charitably in complete selflessness, gentleness and patience. Do all you can to preserve the unity of the Spirit by the peace that binds you together. . . . Work for the Lord with untiring effort and with great earnestness of spirit. If you have hope, this will make you cheerful. Do not give up if trials come; and keep on praying. . . . Think of God's mercy, my brothers and sisters, and worship him, I beg you . . . by offering your living bodies as a holy s a c r i - fice, truly pleasing to God.

Each one of us, however, has been given his own share of grace, (his own special gifts), given as Christ allotted it . . . so that (all of us) together make a unity in the work of service, building up the body of Christ. . . . Just as each of our bodies has several parts and each part has a

separate function, so all of us, in union with Christ, form one body, and as parts of it we belong to each other. In the one Spirit we were all baptized . . . and one Spirit was given to us all to drink. Our gifts differ according to the grace given us. . . .

Ephesians 4: 1 -3, 7;12-13
Romans 12:1,4-6, 11 - 12;
1 Corinthians 12:13

Reconciliation

When we are going through times of suffering, diminished capacity and function due to illness, or confinement as a shut-in, we often feel worthless, isolated, lonely, and unable to contribute to others. We may feel separated from God, from our church community or cut off from life. We are not alone. The Lord is with us always. In his Body, the Church, we are united with one another.

Pray to the Lord about any feelings you may have of separation from him or from others. Share with him your loneliness, isolation or depression. Tell him about anything that makes you feel hopeless, useless, empty, or devoid of having anything to give. . . . Ask the Lord for his help and his healing. Let him embrace you with his love.

Meditation

Each one of us is very dear and very precious to the Lord. Each of us has our own sacred dignity and worth, our own call to holiness. Regardless of our condition, each of us has been given special gifts from the Lord with which we can serve him and each other. When we can no longer be active physically, we need to become more active spiritually, leading a more contemplative life. Even if we are bedridden, we can bring the Lord's love to others in our own special way. Offering our prayers and suffering to the Lord can be a source of redemption for ourselves, our loved ones, our Church and indeed, the whole world.

Take some time now to meditate on your special gifts and talents with which you could serve the Lord and others. Ask the Lord to reveal to you your special vocation, your special ministry. Thank and praise him for the gifts and charisms he has given you.

Scripture Reading

May the God of our Lord Jesus Christ, the Father of glory, give you a spirit of wisdom and perception of what is revealed, to bring you to full knowledge of him. May he enlighten the eyes of your mind so that you can see what hope his call holds for you, what rich glories he has promised . . . and how infinitely great is the power that he has exercised for us believers. . . . He has put all things under his feet, and made him, as the ruler of everything, the head of the Church, which is his body, the fullness of him who fills the whole creation. . . . It is by grace that you have been saved, through faith; not by anything of your own, but by a gift from God; not by anything that you have done, so that nobody can claim the credit. We are God's work of art, created in Christ Jesus to live the good life as from the beginning he had meant us to live it.

—Ephesians 1:17-19, 22-23; 2:8-10

Gospel

Later on, Jesus showed himself again to the disciples. It was by the Sea of Tiberias, and it happened like this . . . It was light by now and there stood Jesus on the shore. . . . Jesus said to them, "Come and have breakfast." None of the disciples was bold enough to ask, "Who are you?"; they knew quite well it was the Lord. Jesus then stepped forward, took the bread and gave it to them, and the same with the fish. This was the third time that Jesus showed himself to the disciples after rising from the dead.

After the meal Jesus said to Simon Peter, "Simon son of John, do you love me more than these others do?" He answered, "Yes, Lord, you know I love you." Jesus said to him, "Feed my lambs." A second time he said to him, "Simon son of John, do you love me?" He replied, "Yes Lord, you know I love you." Jesus said to him, "Look after my sheep." Then he said to him a third time, "Simon son of John, do you love me?" Peter was upset that he asked him the third time, "Do you love me?" and said, "Lord, you know everything; you know I love you." Jesus said to him, "Feed my sheep."

— John 21:1, 4, 12-17

Prayer

Dear Lord, you promised to be with us always. Give us an awareness of your abiding presence. We need you. Be our strength when we are weak. Fill our emptiness with yourself. In your loving wisdom and compassion you said, "It is not good for man to be alone." In times of loneliness and depression, unite us with our spiritual family in you. Comfort us with the presence of those special people in our lives with whom we can share your love.

Help us, dear Lord, to recognize the special gifts you have given us, our special talents. Show us the special things we can do to build up your Body, our special vocation, regardless of our circumstances. Nourish us with your love so that we, in turn, can nourish others by sharing your love and healing with them. Let us be powerful instruments in your hands so that we too can, each in our own way, "Take care of your lambs" and "Feed your sheep."

Our Father . . .

Communion or Quiet Prayer

After Communion

You did not choose me, no, I chose you; and I commissioned you to go out and to bear fruit, fruit that will last; and then the Father will give you anything you ask him in my name. What I command you is to love one another.

— John 15:16-17

14

Mary,
Our Mother

The word that was addressed to Jeremiah by Yahweh, "Get up and make your way down to the potter's house; there I shall let you hear what I have to say." So I went down to the potter's house; and there he was, working at the wheel. And whenever the vessel he was making came out wrong, as happens with the clay handled by potters, he would start afresh and work it into another vessel, as potters do. Then this word of Yahweh was addressed to me, "House of Israel, can not I do to you what this potter does?—it is Yahweh who speaks. Yes, as the clay is in the potter's hand, so you are in mine. . . ."

— Jeremiah 18:1-6

Reconciliation

Come to quiet before the Lord. . . . Open yourself to the help and guidance of the Holy Spirit. Share with the Lord anything that may prevent you from surrendering yourself to him. Tell him about any fears or misgivings you may have about his will for you. Share with him any inability to trust him. Remain still in the Lord's presence and allow him to do whatever he wants in you.

Prayer

Dear Mary, Our Mother, you surrendered yourself to the Lord in total self-giving. You shared his suffering, as well as sharing in his glory. Help us to trust the Lord, so that we too can give ourselves completely into his hands. Help us to believe, as you did, that all things are possible with God. In times of trial and darkness, inspire us with a deep faith in the Lord's providential care.

In spite of our unworthiness, you love us as Jesus loves us, with tenderness and mercy. You are our Mother, too. Help us to grow in love for the Lord. You were the first person on earth to be one with Jesus. Show us how to have an intimate relationship with Our Lord. Help us to become truly holy, as you are holy.

Scripture Reading

. . . The angel Gabriel was sent by God to a town in Galilee called Nazareth, to a virgin betrothed to a man named Joseph, of the House of David; and the virgin's name was Mary. He went in and said to her, "Rejoice, so highly favored! The Lord is with you." She was deeply disturbed by these words and asked herself what this greeting could mean, but the angel said to her, "Mary, do not be afraid; you have won God's favor. Listen! You are to conceive and bear a son, and you must name him Jesus. He will be great and will be called Son of the Most High. The Lord God will give him the throne of his ancestor David; he will rule over the House of Jacob for ever and his reign will have no end."

Mary said to the angel, "But how can this come about, since I am a virgin?" "The Holy Spirit will come upon you," the angel answered, "and the power of the Most High will cover you with its shadow. And so the child will be holy and will be called Son of God. Know this too: your kinswoman Elizabeth has, in her old age, herself conceived a son, and she whom people called barren is now in her sixth month, for nothing is impossible to God." "I am the handmaid of the Lord," said Mary, "let what you have said be done to me." And the angel left her.

—Luke 1:26-38

Responsorial Psalm

Luke 1:46-55

R: **I trust in you, O Lord; my life is in your hands.**
My soul proclaims the greatness of the Lord
and my spirit exults in God my savior;
because he has looked upon his lowly handmaid.

R: **I trust in you, O Lord; my life is in your hands.**
Yes, from this day forward all generations will call me
blessed,
for the Almighty has done great things for me.
Holy is his name,
and his mercy reaches from age to age for those who
fear him.

R: I trust in you, O Lord; my life is in your hands.

He has shown the power of his arm,

he has routed the proud of heart.

He has pulled down princes from their thrones and

exalted the lowly.

The hungry he has filled with good things, the rich

sent empty away.

R: I trust in you, O Lord; my life is in your hands.

He has come to the help of . . . his servant, mindful of

his mercy—

according to the promise he made to our ancestors of

his mercy to Abraham and to his descendants for

ever.

R: I trust in you, O Lord; my life is in your hands.

Gospel

Near the cross of Jesus stood his mother and his mother's sister, Mary the wife of Clopas, and Mary of Magdala. Seeing his mother and the disciple he loved standing near her, Jesus said to his mother, "Woman, this is your son." Then to the disciple he said, "This is your mother." And from that moment the disciple made a place for her in his home.

— John 19:25-27

Meditation

As Jesus was dying, he gave Mary to John to be his mother. So too does the Lord give Mary to us to be our Mother. We need not be afraid to let Mary draw close to us. She loves us as a mother loves her precious child. She fully shared in our humanity. From her own experience, she understands the pain and suffering of life. Just as Mary shared in our Lord's suffering, so too will she stand by us in our tribulations. Let us not hesitate to go to her with our needs.

We need not be ashamed of our unworthiness before our Mother. She wishes only to help us and to participate in our healing and redemption. She is the Mediatrix of grace. Let us open ourselves to receive whatever grace our Blessed Mother wants to give us, so that we may become like her in holiness and oneness with our Lord.

Our Father . . .

Communion or Quiet Prayer

After Communion

. . . Here God lives among men. He will make his home among them; they shall be his people, and he will be their God; his name is God-with-them. He will wipe away all tears from their eyes; there will be no more death, and no more mourning or sadness. The world of the past has gone. . . . Now I [the Lord] am making [all things] new.

—Revelation 21:3-5

111

Acknowledgments

Photo Credits:
  Algimantas Kezys
  Chapters 5,6,7,8,9,11,12

  George A. Lane, S.J.
  Chapters 1,2,3,4,10,13,14